The Seminole

Liz Sonneborn

Watts LIBRARY

Franklin Watts
A Division of Scholastic Inc.
New York • Toronto • London • Auckland • Sydney
Mexico City • New Delhi • Hong Kong
Danbury, Connecticut

Note to readers: Definitions for words in **bold** can be found in the Glossary at the back of this book.

Photographs © 2001: AP/Wide World Photos: 44; Art Resource, NY/Smithsonian American Art Museum, Washington, DC: cover reference; Corbis-Bettmann: 52 (Tony Arruza), 30, 31 (Tom Bean), 32 (Gianni Dagli Orti), 22; Florida State Archives: 27; National Geographic Image Collection/Willard R. Culver: 43; North Wind Picture Archives: 3 right, 6, 17, 20, 21; Oklahoma Historical Society, Archives & Manuscripts Division: 3 left, 33, 37, 45; Raymond Bial: 28, 29, 40, 42; Stock Montage, Inc.: 8, 11 (The Newberry Library), 14; Sun Valley Video & Photography: 18, 19, 38, 39, 49, 50, 51 (Marilyn "Angel" Wynn), 46 (The Creative Source), 13, 24, 26, 41; Viesti Collection, Inc./Morgan Williams: 9.

Cover illustration by Gary Overacre, based on a photograph © Art Resource, NY/Smithsonian American Art Museum, Washington, DC.

Map by XNR Productions Inc.

Library of Congress Cataloging-in-Publication Data

Sonneborn, Liz
    The Seminole / by Liz Sonneborn
        p. cm — (Watts Library)
    Includes bibliographical references and index.
    ISBN 0-531-13951-4 (lib. bdg.)   0-531-16228-1 (pbk.)
    1. Seminole Indians—Juvenile literature. [1. Seminole Indians. 2. Indians of North America—Southern states.] I. Title. II. Series.
E99 .S28 S48 2002
975.9'004973–dc21

                                                  2001017966

Contents

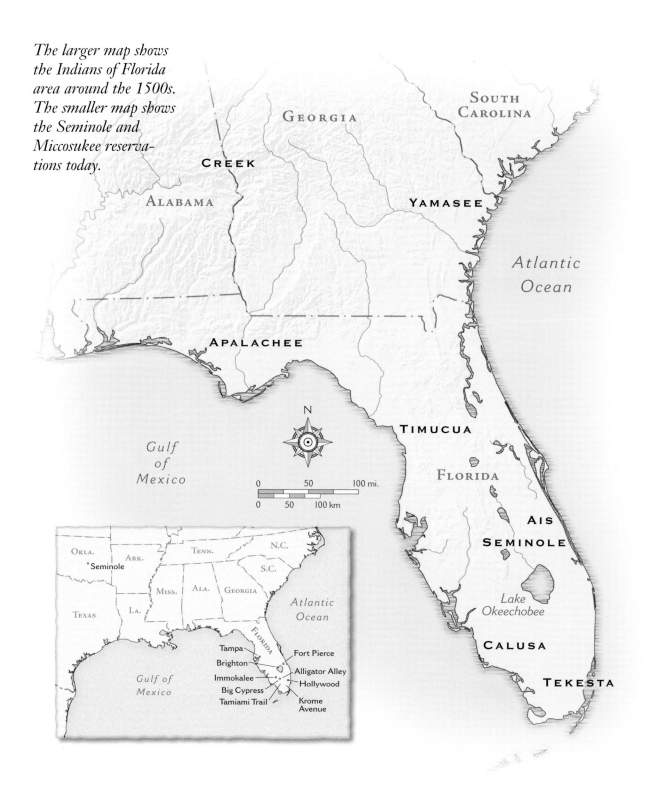

The larger map shows the Indians of Florida area around the 1500s. The smaller map shows the Seminole and Miccosukee reservations today.

SOUTH CAROLINA

GEORGIA

CREEK

ALABAMA

YAMASEE

Atlantic Ocean

APALACHEE

Gulf of Mexico

N

0   50   100 mi.
0   50   100 km

TIMUCUA

FLORIDA

AIS

SEMINOLE

Lake Okeechobee

CALUSA

TEKESTA

OKLA.   TENN.   N.C.
•Seminole   ARK.   S.C.
TEXAS   LA.   MISS.   ALA.   GEORGIA
                              Atlantic Ocean
                    FLORIDA
            Tampa   Fort Pierce
            Brighton   Alligator Alley
Gulf of   Immokalee   Hollywood
Mexico   Big Cypress
            Tamiami Trail   Krome Avenue

Chapter One

Living in the Southeast

The Seminole Indians are made up of many different peoples. During the early 1700s, the tribe came into being when Creek Indians from Georgia and Alabama moved into Florida. There, they were joined by Indians of other southeastern groups, such as the Yamasee and Apalachee. Together, these people became known as the Seminole.

The tribes that composed the Seminole first encountered Europeans in the 1500s. Before then, they shared similar ways of life that took advantage of their mild climate and lush environment. They lived well by farming its rich soil, hunting in its thick forests, and fishing in its fresh streams and rivers.

Farmers and Hunters

The Indians of the Southeast obtained most of their food by farming. They grew crops in small gardens near their houses and in large fields shared by entire villages. Together, men and women cleared the land, usually by burning down all the trees on a plot. Their best farmland was found along well-watered riverbeds.

Women were responsible for planting seeds and tending crops. They planted beans, squash, and pumpkins, but their

Southeastern Indian women helped to feed their people by growing crops, such as corn, beans, and squash.

21

most important crop was corn. Women made dozens of corn dishes, including corn mush and corn bread. These dishes were often flavored with onions, berries, nuts, and other wild plants the women gathered. Any leftover corn they dried and stored in baskets they wove from cane and other plant materials. With stored corn, the Indians of the Southeast never had to worry about going hungry.

Men contributed to the food supply by hunting. A talented hunter was treated with great respect, so young men were always eager to go on their first hunt. Using spears, knives, and bows and arrows, the Indians hunted large animals, such as bear and deer. Working in groups, hunters sometimes set a fire in the woods to drive deer into a corral, where they could easily slay the trapped herd.

Hunters used clubs and darts shot from blowguns to kill smaller animals and birds. Rabbits, raccoons, turkeys, and ducks all made hearty meals. Men also fished with hooks they made from bone, shell, and antlers. In another popular way of fishing, men placed a natural poison into standing pools of water to stun the fish swimming there. They and their families could make an impressive catch simply by scooping up the groggy fish with their hands.

Women cooked the meat and fish their husbands brought home into tasty stews. They also skinned the slaughtered deer and turned their hides into leather by soaking them in a mixture of water and animal brains. From the leather, women fashioned loincloths for the men in their family and skirts for

Hunting Alligators

Timucua hunters stunned alligators by ramming spears into their mouths and then killed them with clubs and arrows.

Keeping Cool

During the long, hot summer, southeastern Indian children usually wore no clothing at all.

themselves. They also sewed bags and moccasins, which the Indians used while traveling. And, in the winter, they wore robes made of warm animal fur.

Village Life

Because they relied on their farm crops, southeastern Indians had to stay close to their fields to tend them properly. As a result, they lived in permanent villages. The smallest ones housed about one hundred people. The largest villages had populations of more than one thousand.

A village was made up of as many as one hundred houses. They were clustered around an open square, where the people

This illustration shows a Florida Indian village in the mid-1500s.

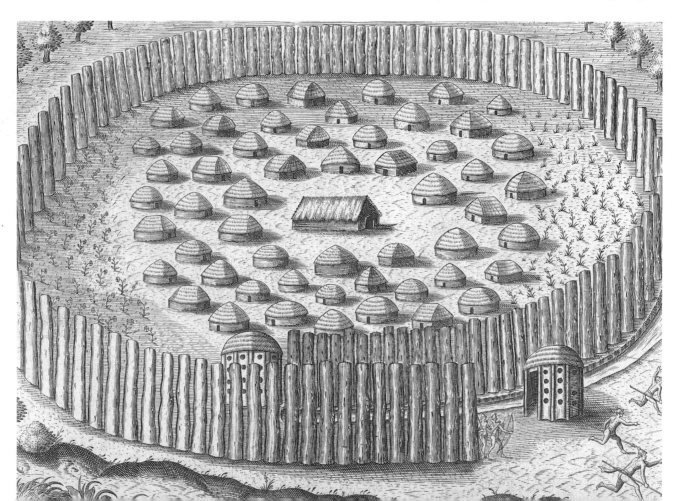

of the village gathered for ceremonies and feasts. To keep out intruders, some villages were surrounded by a high fence made of tree trunks stuck into the ground.

Each family had two houses—one for winter and one for summer. Both were built from tree trunks and branches covered with roofs made of grass, branches, and bark. In the summer house, the sides were left open to allow cool breezes to flow through.

Most members of a household belonged to the same **clan**. A clan was a group of people who were descended from the same ancestor. Clans usually were named after animals, such as the deer, bear, bird, and snake.

A man and a woman of the same clan were forbidden to marry each other. For instance, a Deer man could marry a Bird woman or a Bear woman, but never a Deer woman. Clan elders arranged most marriages, but either the bride or the groom could object to a match.

Before a couple could be married, the groom had to give gifts to the bride's family. These presents proved that he would be a good provider. If the family accepted the gifts, the groom moved into his bride's family home or built a new house nearby.

Children belonged to their mother's clan. Although their fathers loved and

A man had to prove to his future bride's family that he could take good care of her before they would be allowed to marry.

9

supported them, children were primarily raised by their mothers and her male relatives. Girls learned how to do women's work from their mothers, while boys were instructed in men's work by their mothers' brothers. If children misbehaved, they were often punished by having their body scratched with a wood or bone tool. However, the scratches were not as painful as the shame the children felt when other villagers saw the scratches and knew they had misbehaved.

Very successful hunters or warriors sometimes took a second or even a third wife. The first wife, though, was always considered the most important. Because the new wives were usually her sisters or cousins, the first wife welcomed them into her family. And, as the wives of a wealthy man, all were given special respect within their village.

Leading the People

The most important person in a village was the **micco**, or chief, who often inherited his position. He organized feasts, managed the shared fields, and helped decide when the village

Black Drink

During council meetings, village leaders drank a sacred medicine called **black drink**. It was a tea made from the leaves and stems of the holly plant. The council members passed around a large conch shell filled with the medicine. Each member took a sip, then handed the shell to the next. They believed this black drink purified the body, soothed anger, and helped people speak truthfully.

should go to war. The micco was aided by a council of older men and respected warriors.

Each village also had a war chief. He was responsible for organizing war parties. Southeastern Indians went to war for several reasons. They might want to avenge a raid staged by another group or take war captives, whom they could turn into slaves. Sometimes villages went to war merely because the men wanted to show their bravery. Earning a reputation as a skilled and courageous warrior gave a man great influence among his people.

A war chief meets with warriors to prepare for battle.

Tattoos of War

Successful warriors earned the right to tattoo their bodies. They wore these tattoos proudly—like badges of honor.

Before going to war, men purified their bodies by fasting and spending time in **sweat lodges**. Inside these structures, men sat around a bed of stones that were heated in a fire and then sprinkled with water. The steam that rose from the stones caused the men to sweat heavily. With the sweat, harmful pollutants in their bodies were drawn out.

Other villagers also performed rituals, guided by powerful medicine men. These people were respected and feared because they had a special understanding of the spirit world. When the spirits were unhappy, bad things would happen. Holding ceremonies that honored the spirits, therefore, was important for the well-being of the village.

Many medicine men were well trained as healers. They used herbs to make medicines and held rituals to cure illness. Medicine men also performed ceremonies to control weather, ensure a successful hunt, and even improve a person's love life.

For the Indians of the Southeast, the most important ceremony was the **Green Corn Dance**. It was a ritual held in late summer when the corn crop had ripened. During the first days of the ceremony, men purified themselves in sweat lodges and gathered to discuss matters of concern to the village. One topic of discussion was the fate of those people who had committed crimes during the previous year. For minor crimes, people might be beaten or fined. Murderers, however, might be executed or told to leave the village forever.

During the Green Corn Dance, women cleaned their houses and put out their household fires. Likewise, the leading

medicine man extinguished the fire that burned inside the building where the village council met. This holy man then relit the fire, and the women used its coals to set new fires in their homes. With this ceremony, the old year ended and a new year began. It was followed by a great feast, during which the villagers sang and danced. Old wrongs were forgiven, and old friendships were renewed. Dancing with their friends and family, the Indians thanked the spirits and celebrated as their world was born anew.

This drawing shows Seminole Indians participating in the Green Corn Dance.

The arrival of Spanish explorer Juan Ponce de León and his expedition caused much suffering for the Florida Indians.

Chapter Two

Becoming the Seminole

Before the 1500s, about 100,000 Indians lived in Florida. However, their lives changed forever in 1513. In that year, Spanish explorer Juan Ponce de León and his men became the first Europeans to come to the area. Florida Indians were far from welcoming to these newcomers. They battled the Spaniards and killed Ponce de León with an arrow to the thigh in 1521.

Even so, Spanish explorers continued to travel to Florida. The Spanish could

Deadly Encounters

Soon after their first contact with Spaniards, about half the Indians in Florida lost their lives to disease.

fight off their Indian enemies because they had guns—far more deadly weapons than bows and arrows. But the Indians faced an even greater threat from the Spaniards—European diseases. The Spaniards carried germs of diseases such as measles and smallpox. Indians had never been exposed to these germs, so, unlike the Spanish, their bodies had no **immunities** to them. A Spaniard who caught measles would feel slightly ill and then recover, but when an Indian who was exposed to measles almost always died.

The Runaway Tribe

In the beginning of the 1600s, settlers from England also began to arrive in the Southeast. North of Florida, they built large farms called **plantations**. To work their fields, the English needed many laborers. Some Englishmen began raiding villages to take Indian prisoners, whom they made their slaves. Strong Indian groups soon began attacking weaker ones to obtain captives they could trade to English colonists. Florida Indians were particularly vulnerable because the Spaniards would not allow them to have guns. They were clearly no match for northern tribes armed by the English. Because of disease and slavery, Florida tribes such as the Timucua and Calusa had almost died out by the early 1700s.

Other tribes soon moved into the lands where these people once lived. Most of the newcomers had been members of the Muscogee Nation (also known as the Creek Nation), a powerful people who had lived in Georgia and

The Seminole Name

The name *Seminole* came from the Spanish word *cimarrón,* meaning "wild" or "runaway."

16

Alabama. Runaway black slaves formed other communities nearby. The English had brought these slaves from Africa to work on their plantations.

Runaway slaves settled near the Muscogee in Florida.

These Indians slowly formed a new people, whom Europeans called the Seminole. They farmed, hunted, and lived in villages, just as southeastern Indians had for hundreds of years. Over time, however, they took on new ways. They began using metal tools and cloth they obtained from Europeans through trade. They also began to grow melons and oranges and raise cows and pigs—crops and animals introduced to them by the Spaniards. Their ability to combine the old and the new made the Seminole a resourceful and powerful people.

Fighting Jackson

In 1775, English settlers—now calling themselves Americans—began fighting for their independence from England. They won the war in 1783 and formed the United States. Some southeastern Indians, including many Muscogee, were disturbed by these developments. They had allied themselves to the English, so they considered the Americans to be their enemies. In 1812, when the United States and England again went to war, many Muscogee sided with the English. The next year, they attacked and killed 500 Americans and American-allied Muscogee at Fort Mims, a post near what is now Mobile, Alabama. The U.S. Army then went to war against the Muscogee. More than 800 Muscogee warriors were killed, and many of their villages were destroyed. The tribe admitted defeat in 1814, and the United States took over much of their land. To

escape American control, thousands of Muscogee fled to Florida and joined the Seminole. These newcomers doubled the size of the tribe, making the Seminole stronger than ever.

During the war, the Seminole had their own problems with Americans. Plantation owners were angry that many of their

This photograph shows a re-enactment of an 1812 battle at the Big Cypress reservation in Florida.

U.S. soldiers capture several Indian chiefs in the First Seminole War.

runaway African slaves had found a home with the Seminole. They claimed the Seminole had stolen their slaves, and they hired men to enter Seminole territory and capture the runaways. When the Seminole fought these intruders, the United States declared war against the tribe.

In 1817, U.S. troops headed into Florida to punish the Seminole. Florida was then considered Spanish territory, so the military action was a violation of international law. However, there were so few Spaniards in Florida that they could do little to resist the invading army.

The Seminole fought hard, but they were greatly outnumbered. Americans led by General Andrew Jackson were able to drive them from their lands. The Seminole fled south, where they hid out in the swampland. By 1818, the Seminole had lost what became known as the **First Seminole War**. Though defeated, the Seminole had sent a message that they were fighters, determined to battle to the death to keep their homeland.

Original.

Treaty

Of Amity, Settlement and Limits

between

the United States of America, and His Catholic Majesty

The United States of America and His Catholic Majesty desiring to consolidate on a permanent basis the friendship and good correspondence which happily prevails between the two Parties, have determined to settle and terminate all their differences and pretensions by a Treaty, which shall designate with precision the Limits of their respective bordering territories in North America.

With this intention the President of the United States has furnished with their full Powers John Quincy Adams, Secretary of State of the said United States, and His Catholic Majesty has appointed the Most Excellent Lord Don Luis de Onis, Gonzales, Lopez y Vara, Lord of the town of Rayaces, Perpetual Regidor of the Corporation of the City of Salamanca, Knight Grand Cross of the Royal American Order of Isabella, the Catholick, decorated with the Lys of La Vendee, Knight Pensioner of the Royal and distinguished Spanish Order Charles the third, Member of the Supreme Assembly of the said Royal Order; of the Council of His Catholic Majesty; his Secretary with exercise of decrees and his Envoy Extraordinary and Minister Plenipotentiary near the United States of America.

And the said Plenipotentiaries after having exchanged their Powers, have agreed upon and concluded the following Articles.

Article 1.

There shall be a firm and inviolable Peace and sincere Friendship between the United States and their Citizens and His Catholic Majesty, his Successors and Subjects without exception of persons or places.

Chapter Three

The Second Seminole War

The U.S. Army's invasion of Florida showed Spain how hard it would be to keep control over their lands in the Southeast. Rather than go to war for it, Spain decided to sell Florida to the United States in 1821. With the purchase, the Seminole found themselves living on lands their American enemies now considered their own.

American settlers were soon eyeing the Seminole's best farmland. The settlers pressured politicians to get the

Seminole out of Florida once and for all. Governor William P. Duval of Florida responded by inviting seventy Seminole leaders to a council in 1823. Duval tried to persuade them to move to Georgia to live among the Muscogee, but the Seminole thought the idea was absurd. Though they were related to the Muscogee, they now thought of them as enemies. Besides, the Seminole considered themselves an independent tribe. They had no interest in joining another Indian people.

Governor Duval was not happy with Neamathla, a Seminole chief who advised his people against moving from their homelands.

Under pressure, some of the Seminole chiefs, however, agreed to another plan. In the Treaty of Moultrie Creek, they said the tribe would move from northern Florida to a large **reservation** in the center of the state. The United States promised that no settlers would disturb them in their new lands. In return, the Seminole pledged not to take in any more runaway slaves.

The Removal Threat

From the start, the arrangement was a disaster for the Seminole. Their reservation land was too sandy to grow healthy crops, so they were constantly hungry. Adding to their troubles, whites kept invading their lands to capture runaway slaves, and the U.S. government did nothing to stop them.

The Seminole's situation grew even worse in 1830. That year, their old enemy Andrew Jackson was elected president. He supported **Removal**, the relocation of southeastern Indians to lands in the West. Once the Indians were gone, Jackson planned to open up their old homelands to settlement by white Americans.

The Seminole became one of the first targets for Removal. Weakened by war and famine, some were too tired to resist. Others refused to leave Florida. They had already moved once to please whites, and they were not willing to move again.

In 1832, seven Seminole chiefs traveled west to the Indian country. This area included land in present-day Oklahoma where the United States wanted to relocate the tribe. There, they signed the Treaty of Fort Gibson. In it, they agreed that all the Seminole people would move to the Indian country. These chiefs, however, had no right to speak for the entire tribe. When the Seminole found out about the agreement, many felt angry and betrayed by the Americans.

Back at War

The United States told the Seminole they would have to set out for the Indian country at the beginning of 1836. Just months before the deadline, the Seminole began attacking

Seminole warriors launch an attack against a U.S. fort in 1837 during the Second Seminole War.

Osceola

The most famous leader of the Seminole, Osceola led the tribe's fight against the U.S. Army in the Second Seminole War (1835–42). As a young man, he declared he would resist any effort to drive the Seminole from their Florida homeland. During treaty negotiations in 1823, many tribal leaders agreed to move to western lands. But Osceola firmly refused.

Osceola proved just as determined on the battlefield. During the war, he led the Seminole in a series of battles against U.S. troops. While fighting, however, Osceola fell seriously ill with **malaria.** Exhausted and sick, he agreed to attend peace talks with American officials. The Americans betrayed him and took him captive. Three months later, the mighty Osceola died in prison at the age of about thirty-four.

Cooacoochee had been a prisoner during part of the war until he escaped in 1837.

white settlements and U.S. Army posts in Florida. The raids set off a bloody conflict that became known as the **Second Seminole War** (1835–42).

American soldiers met the Seminole raids with their own violent actions. The soldiers burned the Seminole villages and fields and took their women and children hostage. Twice, Seminole leaders who tried to negotiate with U.S. officials were taken captive and thrown in prison. One was the great war chief Osceola (also known as Asin Yahola), who inspired many other Indian warriors with his determination to remain in Florida or die.

After Osceola's death in 1838, Cooacoochee—also known as Wild Cat—took over his role as the resistance leader. After three years of brutal warfare, Cooacoochee felt he had no choice but to surrender. By that

The Longest War

The Second Seminole War was the longest, most expensive war the United States has ever fought.

time, thousands of the exhausted Seminole had already left their homes and moved to the West.

A few hundred, however, refused to give up. They retreated into the **Everglades**, a great swamp in southern Florida. In that dark, dank swamp, it was almost impossible for U.S. soldiers to find them. Frustrated, the Americans slowly gave up the fight. On August 14, 1842, the United States declared the war was over. The small band of Seminole left in Florida had effectively beaten the U.S. Army. In addition to the humiliation of defeat, the United States had lost about 1,500 soldiers and spent more than $20 million.

The Seminole, however, had also paid a high price. They were now a divided people. About 4,000 Seminole lived in the **Indian country**, while some 500 remained in southern Florida. Both the western and eastern Seminole had been torn from their homes. Each group now faced the challenge of remaking their world in an unfamiliar—and unfriendly—environment.

Some of the Seminole hid in the Everglades rather than surrender to U.S. forces.

The Seminole people struggled in Indian country to grow crops and to survive the difficult winters and summers.

Chapter Four

The Seminole Nation in the West

The Seminole who moved to the Indian country in the 1830s and 1840s found themselves in a new world. In the Southeast, they had enjoyed a comfortable life. Their rich fields and thick forests had always provided plenty of vegetables and meat to eat. They also had a mild climate, with summery weather for most of the year.

Their lands in the Indian country proved far less inviting. The land was difficult to farm. They had to work much harder in their fields to grow less food. The weather also was harsh. The western Seminole had to brave bitter cold in the winter and steaming temperatures in the summer. In their early years in the West, many tribal members died of hunger and disease.

Chief Micanopy helped the Seminole gain a bit of land in Indian country.

Making a Nation

To make matters worse, the Seminole had no lands to call their own. U.S. officials told them to live in the territory of the Muscogee—people the Seminole considered their enemies. The Muscogee were also a much larger Indian group. The Seminole feared that if they lived among them, their people would eventually become more like Muscogee and less like Seminole. The situation threatened their very future as a people.

A group of Seminole led by Micanopy refused to live among the Muscogee, however. They settled near Fort Gibson, a U.S. Army post in the Cherokee Nation. The U.S. government worried that if they forced the Seminole to leave the fort, war might break out. Finally, in 1845, the United States agreed in a treaty that the Seminole could live separately from the Muscogee. Yet, the Seminole still did not have a true nation of their own.

Not satisfied with life among Americans and the Muscogee, Cooacoochee took his followers to Mexico in 1849. His people worked out a treaty with Mexico to serve in the Mexican army in return for land. A community of African-Americans went with them to escape slavery.

Hoping to improve the lives of the Seminole who remained in the Indian country, Chief John Jumper wrote to President Franklin Pierce in 1853. He helped convince the

In a letter to President Pierce, Chief John Jumper asked for a separate territory for the Seminole.

U.S. government to establish a separate territory for the Seminole. In 1856, the United States recognized the Seminole's claim to 2 million acres (809,375 hectares) west of the Muscogee Nation. Over the next five years, the Seminole slowly moved into this area. Some were hesitant to relocate there, however. They were afraid of the Plains Indians who lived nearby. These peoples, whose lives were centered around hunting and warring, seemed wild and hostile to the settled Seminole.

War and Hard Times

Despite their fears, the Seminole began rebuilding their society in their new home. Their efforts, however, were soon interrupted when the Civil War (1861–65) began. This conflict pitted the states in the North (called the Union) against the states in the South (called the Confederacy). The Seminole, like many other Indian tribes, found themselves reluctantly pulled into this war between two groups of Americans.

In August 1861, representatives of the Confederacy visited the Seminole. They wanted the tribe to sign a treaty, vowing loyalty to their side. By this time, the Seminole were already in a difficult position. In previous treaties, the United States had promised to provide military support to the tribe. But when the Civil War began, it pulled all its troops out of the Indian country. Left unprotected, the Seminole were afraid the Confederacy would attack them if they did not become Confederate allies.

Reluctantly, the Seminole signed a treaty with the Confederacy. About one-third of the tribe's members disagreed with the decision. They fled north to Kansas, where many fought for the Union. As fighting erupted in the Indian country, the Confederate-allied Seminole escaped to the south to Texas. Both groups suffered horribly during the war. Homeless and hungry, many died of disease. In the meantime, their lands were overrun by soldiers and gangs of robbers. By 1865, when the Union won the war, their houses and lands were destroyed.

A Brutal War

About one-fourth of the western Seminole died during the Civil War.

Although many Seminole had fought for the Union, the tribe was forced to sign a punishing peace treaty. They had to give up 2 million acres (809,375 ha) of territory and accept a plot one-tenth that size in lands formerly assigned to the Muscogee. Once again, the Seminole set about rebuilding their nation. At first, there were tensions between tribal members who had supported different sides in the war. But over time, these disagreements were forgotten, and the Seminole created a unified government. They wrote a formal constitution in 1871.

In the late 1800s, the Seminole built trading posts and schools. Whites came to their lands to found Christian churches, but most Seminole continued to practice their traditional religion. By 1880, they were living as fourteen separate groups, called bands, including two made up of African-Americans. The United States had forced the Seminole to admit these African-Americans into the tribe in the peace treaty signed after the Civil War.

The Western Seminole Today

Under pressure from the U.S. government, the Seminole agreed to accept **allotments** in 1898. Like most Indian groups, the Seminole had always shared their land. The government, however, wanted them to live on privately owned plots, as white Americans did. The Seminole's land was split up into small plots called allotments, and each was assigned to the head of a family. When allotment was complete, their tribal government was dissolved. In 1901, the western Seminole became citizens of the United States. Six years later, their old lands in the Indian country became part of the new state of Oklahoma.

Many Seminole quickly sold their allotments. Some were tricked into giving their land over to non-Indian swindlers. In less than twenty years, only one-fifth of the allotments assigned to the tribe were still in Seminole hands. Non-Indians swindled the Seminole out of even more land after oil was discovered in Oklahoma in the 1920s.

In the mid-1930s, the Seminole of Oklahoma reorganized their government according to new guidelines set out by the U.S. government. This did little to keep young Seminole people in their old tribal lands, however. In the mid-1900s, many left their families to find jobs in other areas. Those who remained in Oklahoma increasingly adopted non-Indian ways. The western Seminole now live in modern houses, and most work for wages in industries such as construction and manufacturing. The tribal government also operates several

Wewoka

The Seminole's western capital was called *Wewoka*. The name, meaning "barking water," referred to a noisy waterfall nearby.

successful businesses, including a trading post, bingo parlor, and gaming center. The majority of tribal members are Christians, though many retain their traditional religious beliefs.

In 1990, the Seminole in Oklahoma were awarded $40 million from the U.S. government. The money was compensation for Florida lands that were illegally taken from them in the early 1800s. The tribal government is using the award to provide aid for the elderly, offer scholarships for college and job training, and fund many other programs to benefit the more than 12,000 western Seminole.

Today, the western Seminole live modern lives while still preserving their cultural heritage. Here, a woman and her two children wear traditional clothing for a festival.

Living in the Everglades presented many challenges for the Seminole.

Chapter Five

Life in the Swampland

Like their relatives in the West, the Seminole in Florida had to adapt to a new environment during the late 1800s. After the Second Seminole War (1835–1842), they retreated into the swamps to the south of their old territory. The environment was hardly welcoming—much of the marshy ground was covered with a thin layer of water. The Seminole settled in the few elevated areas that usually remained dry. But even there, they found little good farmland. Unable to grow

The Chickee

In the late 1800s, the Florida Seminole invented a new type of house—the **chickee**, which was built from the leaves and wood of the palmetto tree. The floors of chickees were constructed several feet above the ground to protect the inhabitants from swamp water and snakes. Because the climate was hot year-round, chickees had leaf roofs but no walls. The open structure let families enjoy cool breezes while shading them from the sun.

much food, they came to rely on wild plants and hunting for most of their diet.

The Third Seminole War

While the Florida Seminole were learning to live in their new home, they were largely left alone by non-Indians. Their settlements were hard to reach. It was also so hard to live on their land that few whites had any interest in taking it over. Still, the Seminole well remembered their wars with the U.S. Army. Understandably, they were distrustful of any whites they encountered.

In 1855, a team of surveyors set out to map the Seminole's territory. They infuriated the Seminole by destroying a small field tended by Chief Billy Bowlegs. Bowlegs's followers attacked and injured several of the surveyors. The attack prompted the U.S. Army once again to wage war on the tribe. This conflict—known as the **Third Seminole War** (1855–58)—ended with the Seminole's defeat. Billy Bowlegs and 162 other Seminole agreed to leave Florida and move to the Indian country.

The Third Seminole War was the last armed conflict between the Florida Seminole and the United States. After the war, the tribe was left in peace to live as they chose. Tribal members settled in small camps, which included several related households. People of different camps, however, often visited one another. Although each camp was run independently, this constant contact kept the Seminole close to one another.

Billy Bowlegs's attack on the U.S. surveyors set off the Third Seminole War.

Seminole Patchwork

In the late 1800s, Seminole women in both the east and west first obtained sewing machines from non-Indian traders. Using this new invention, they created a distinctive style of clothing. They cut brightly colored clothing into long bands and then sewed them together to create what became known as **Seminole patchwork**. For themselves, Seminole women sewed patchwork skirts and capes. For men, they made long shirts that came almost down to the knee. Many Seminole still make patchwork clothing for sale.

Many Seminole also developed ties to non-Indians living nearby. The tribe wanted goods that these people had to trade or sell, such as cloth, metal tools, and guns. Seminole hunters discovered that white traders wanted alligator hides and exotic bird feathers. The traders could resell these items at high prices. Alligator hides were used to make expensive handbags and shoes, while feathers were valued as decoration for women's hats. To obtain money to buy goods, some Seminole also worked as laborers on large farms owned by non-Indians.

Creating the Tribes

In the early 1900s, more and more non-Indians came to live in southern Florida as trains and roads made the area easier to reach. Farmers and ranchers started settling in lands along the coast. Gradually, they moved inland, fencing off lands that had been Seminole hunting grounds. By the 1920s, they were joined by thousands of non-Indians who were attracted by Florida's pleasant climate. Soon, the region became a favorite spot for vacationers from the Northeast.

As non-Indians flooded into southern Florida, the U.S. government created two reservations for the Seminole—Big Cypress and Dania (now called Hollywood)—in 1911. A third reservation, Brighton, was formed in 1935. Non-Indians were

Big Cypress was one of the first Seminole reservations.

not allowed to move into these areas, which were reserved for the Seminole's use. The Seminole, however, were still distrustful of the U.S. government. They were hesitant to leave the swamps and move to the reservations. Many decades would pass before most Seminole lived on these reserved lands.

The arrival of non-Indian tourists, however, quickly had an effect on how the Seminole made a living. They discovered that if they set up small villages in resort towns, tourists would pay to watch them go about their daily chores. Seminole women also earned money by crafting dolls dressed in the colorful patchwork clothing like that they sewed for themselves. Some Seminole men made money by putting on shows during which they wrestled alligators. They became famous for this dangerous profession. Though proud of their courage and the income they earned, alligator wrestlers were often scarred and maimed when they were caught in the animals' great jaws.

As more Seminole moved onto their reservations, they decided they needed an organized government. Following guidelines established by U.S. government, these tribal members wrote a constitution in 1957 and began officially

A Seminole man and woman cast their votes for tribal representatives at the Dania reservation.

calling themselves the **Seminole Tribe of Florida**. The constitution called for the tribe to elect representatives to a council and a board of directors. The council was to organize their dealings with the governments of Florida and the United States. The board was to manage the tribe's business affairs. The tribe developed successful businesses that leased land to large vegetable growers and raised cattle.

One group of Indians distantly related to the Seminole lived in their own settlements along Tamiami Trail, an old Indian trail along U.S. Route 41. In 1962, they decided to organize a tribe of their own. They established their own government and named themselves the **Miccosukee Tribe**. Ever since, the U.S. government has recognized the Seminole and Miccosukee as two separate tribes of Florida Indians.

Betty Mae Jumper

The Seminole council's first female chairperson, Betty Mae Jumper, is also the only Seminole woman known to have been a professional alligator wrestler.

James Billie believes that it is important for the Seminole to maintain their traditions and culture and to stay current with the changing world around them. In this photograph, Billie is shown "gigging," or catching a fish using some type of spear.

Chapter Six

The Florida Seminole and Miccosukee Today

In 1987, James Billie, tribal council chairperson of the Florida Seminole, gave a speech at the grand opening of the tribe's hotel in Tampa. "I don't want to lose the old ways," Billie told the crowd. He then added, "But we can't turn back the clock." Billie's words spoke of the greatest challenge the Seminole and Miccosukee tribes now face—keeping their old ways while living in the modern world.

Today, the Florida Seminole have a population of about 2,000. Most live on their six reservations. In addition to Big Cypress, Brighton, and Hollywood, the tribe was recently granted three new reservations—Fort Pierce, Immokalee, and Tampa. The Miccosukee tribe has about 600 members. Many live on the tribe's Tamiami Trail Reservation near Miami. The Miccosukee also control reserved lands in areas known as Alligator Alley and Krome Avenue.

Working for Tourist Dollars

Like their mothers and fathers before them, many Seminole now work as laborers on large farms or on road-repair crews. Others—particularly older women—continue to make dolls, patchwork clothing, and baskets for sale in tourist shops throughout southern Florida. These items are a source of both income and pride for the craftspeople who make them.

The Seminole also earn money through their many successful tribal businesses. Under the leadership of chairperson Billie, the Seminole in 1977 established a smoke shop that sold cigarettes and other tobacco products. In other stores in Florida, customers have to pay high state sales taxes on cigarettes. But state laws and taxes do not apply on reservation lands. The Seminole, therefore, can sell cigarettes at a much lower price than their competitors.

In 1979, the Seminole became the first Indian tribe to open a high-stakes bingo parlor. Because it was on reservation land, the Seminole believed it did not have to follow Florida's laws regulating gambling. In federal court, the tribe successfully defended its position. The Seminole now operate five bingo halls and casinos. Their success has inspired many other tribal governments to open similar businesses. Gambling establishments are now the largest source of revenue for American Indian tribes throughout the United States.

The Seminole's other business enterprises include a citrus farm, a hotel, an arts and crafts shop, and an airplane factory. The tribe also runs several tourist attractions, including the

At the Billie Swamp Safari Wildfire Park, visitors can take a tour of the swamps on a boat.

Wanted: Alligator Wrestlers

"Wanted: Alligator wrestlers. Must be brave and a risk taker. Males and females OK. No experience needed." The Seminole Okalee Indian Village, a tourist attraction run by the Florida Seminole, placed this curious want ad in 2000. The Seminole have staged shows of alligator wrestling for decades but, recently, few young tribe members have been interested in doing this dangerous job. As the village's chief alligator wrestler Mike Bailey admits, "[The alligators will] kill you in a second."

Billie Swamp Safari Wildlife Park. This 2,000-acre (809-ha) park features a replica of an Indian village where visitors can learn about Seminole life in the 1800s.

Keeping Traditions Alive

Running these businesses, the Seminole have had to interact with non-Indians more than ever. Some elders fear that contact with outsiders will make young Seminole forget their old ways. The tribe's businesses, however, have also helped the Seminole stay a united people. Because of the jobs and money they provide, young people do not have to leave the tribe's reservations in search of work. They can stay in their own communities and still enjoy many benefits of modern life, such as good health care and comfortable houses.

Tribal businesses also fund the Ah-Tah-Thi-Ki Museum, which opened in 1997. The museum offers exhibitions to explain Seminole history and culture to Indians and non-Indians alike. In addition, the Seminole tribe operates the

Ah-Fach-Kee Indian School. There, teachers help preserve Seminole culture by instructing children in the tribe's language and traditions.

Like their Seminole relatives, the Miccosukee have also used business income to help retain their old ways. The tribe runs a restaurant, a gift shop, and a casino—all of which bring tourist dollars into their communities. The Miccosukee also hold an Indian arts festival in the summer and a music festival celebrating ethnic cultures throughout southern Florida in the winter.

This photograph shows one of the many displays at the Ah-Tah-Thi-Ki Museum.

In many ways, the Florida Seminole and the Miccosukee live as their non-Indian neighbors do. The houses they live in, the clothing they wear, the entertainment they enjoy—are all similar to those of other Floridians. Yet, in these Indians, a spirit born from the struggles of their ancestors lives on. In war after war, the U.S. soldiers tried to destroy these peoples, but still they survived. Today, the Seminole and the Miccosukee remember with pride what their ancestors suffered and overcame. Like those before them, they continue to change with the times, while fiercely guarding the old ways—the ways that have kept their peoples strong.

A Miccosukee woman makes a traditional dress to sell to visitors.

Timeline

1513	Spanish explorer Juan Ponce de León and his men become the first Europeans to encounter the Indians of Florida.
c. 1700	Timucua and Calusa Indians of Florida are virtually wiped out by disease and warfare. Muscogee Indians from Georgia and Alabama begin moving into their lands.
1813–14	The Muscogee war against U.S. troops. Thousands of survivors flee to Florida and join the Seminole.
1817–18	The U.S. Army invades Spanish Florida to fight the Seminole in the First Seminole War.
1821	Spain sells Florida to the United States.
1823	Seminole leaders agree to move to a reservation in central Florida in the Treaty of Fort Moultrie.
1832	The Treaty of Fort Gibson requires the Seminole to relocate to lands in Indian country (now Oklahoma).
1835–42	Seminole warriors battle U.S. soldiers in the Second Seminole War. Four thousand Seminole are forced to move west, while five hundred remain in Florida.
1853	The western Seminole are granted their own lands in the Indian country.
1855–58	Billie Bowlegs's band of Florida Seminole fight U.S. troops in the Third Seminole War.
1861	The Seminole in the West pledge allegiance to the Confederacy.
1866	The western Seminole exchange 2 million acres (809,375 ha) for $200,000 in a peace treaty with the United States.

continued on next page

1898	The western Seminole agree to divide their tribal lands into allotments. Their government is later dissolved.
1911	The Florida Seminole are granted the Big Cypress and Dania Reservations.
1935	The Seminole Nation in the West reorganizes its tribal government.
1957	The Seminole Tribe of Florida is recognized by the U.S. government.
1962	The Miccosukee Tribe is recognized by the U.S. government.
1979	The Seminole open the first Indian high-stakes bingo hall in Hollywood, Florida.
1990	The eastern and western Seminole are awarded $40 million in compensation for Florida land.
1997	The Florida Seminole open the Ah-Tah-Thi-Ki Museum.

Glossary

allotment—a plot of reservation land assigned to an individual Indian as privately owned property. The Seminole's lands in the West were divided into allotments in the 1800s.

black drink—a medicinal tea drunk by southeastern Indians to purify their bodies during political meetings and religious ceremonies

chickee—an open-walled house built by the Florida Seminole from the leaves and wood of the palmetto tree

clan—a group of people who believe they were descended from the same distant ancestor

Everglades—a large swampy area in southern Florida

First Seminole War—a conflict during which the U.S. Army invaded Spanish Florida to attack the Seminole in 1817–18

Green Corn Dance—the annual ceremony held by south-eastern Indians to give thanks to the spirits and celebrate the ripening of the year's corn crop

immunities—substances produced by the body to help fight disease-causing germs

Indian country—land in what is now Oklahoma to which most Seminole were forced to relocate in the 1830s and 1840s

malaria—a serious disease spread by mosquitoes

micco—the leader of a Seminole village

Miccosukee Tribe—a group of Indians living along the Tamiami Trail (now U.S. Route 41) in southern Florida who organized their own tribe in 1962

plantation—a large farm, often run with the labor of slaves

Removal—U.S. government policy that sought to relocate southeastern Indians to western lands in present-day Oklahoma

reservation—an area of land set aside for an Indian group by the U.S. government

Second Seminole War—the conflict fought between 1835 and 1842 in which the U.S. Army compelled about four thousand Seminole to move to what is now Oklahoma. Five hundred Seminole hiding in the Everglades were able to stay in Florida.

Seminole patchwork—bands of cloth sewn together in colorful patterns that Seminole women craft into long skirts, capes, and shirts

Seminole Tribe of Florida—the group of Florida Seminole officially recognized as a tribe by the U.S. government in 1957

sweat lodge—a structure in which Indian people sit around a bed of heated stones in order to sweat impurities from their body

Third Seminole War—the conflict between the U.S. Army and the Florida Seminole followers of Billy Bowlegs, fought between 1855 and 1858. After their defeat, Bowlegs's band moved to the Seminole Nation in what is now Oklahoma.

To Find Out More

Books

Jumper, Betty Mae. *Legends of the Seminoles*. Sarasota, FL: Pineapple Press, 1998.

Jumper, Moses and Ben Sonder. *Osceola: Patriot and Warrior*. Austin, TX: Raintree Steck-Vaughn, 1993.

Kavasch, E. Barrie. *Seminole Children and Elders Talk Together*. New York: Rosen Publishing, 1999.

Koslow, Philip. *The Seminole Indians*. New York: Chelsea House, 1994.

Sneve, Virginia Driving Hawk. *The Seminoles*. New York: Holiday House, 1994.

Online Sites

The Miccosukee Tribe
http://www.miccosukeetribe.com
The Miccosukee, an Indian group related to the Seminole but organized as a separate tribe, describe their history, government, and business enterprises.

The Seminole Nation of Oklahoma
http://www.cowboy.net/native/seminole/index.html
This official site about the western Seminole features short articles on their history, as well as historical and modern photographs.

The Seminole Tribe of Florida
http://www.seminoletribe.com
Readers can find all kinds of information on the Florida Seminole's past and present—from photos to legends to recipes—on this site created by the tribe.

A Note on Sources

Good general surveys of Seminole history include Merwyn S. Garbarino's *The Seminole* and James W. Covington's *The Seminoles of Florida*. Jane F. Lancaster's *Removal Aftershock: The Seminoles' Struggles to Survive in the West, 1836–1866* offered me welcome information on the western Seminole's early years in Indian Territory. For the recent history of the Florida Seminole and the Miccosukee, I have relied on Patsy West's *The Enduring Seminoles: From Alligator Wrestling to Ecotourism* and Brent Richards Weisman's *Unconquered People: Florida's Seminole and Miccosukee Indians*. For the eastern Seminole's own take on their past and present, I have also found the tribe's web site (http://www.seminoletribe.com) a valuable resource.

—*Liz Sonneborn*

Index

Numbers in *italics* indicate illustrations.

About the Author

Liz Sonneborn is a writer and an editor, living in Brooklyn, New York. A graduate of Swarthmore College, she specializes in books about the history and culture of American Indians and the biographies of noteworthy people in American history. She has written more than twenty books for children and adults, including *A to Z of Native American Women* and *The New York Public Library's Amazing Native American History*, winner of a Parent's Choice Award.